FEELINGS INTO WORDS

A creative English course/Stage 1

Christopher Copeman and Graham Barrett

Ward Lock Educational

ISBN 0 7062 3465 0

First published 1976
Reprinted 1982

Photographs by Mick Csaky
Design by Paula Hawkins

Set in 12 point Monotype Gill Sans
and printed by The Whitefriars Press Ltd,
London and Tonbridge
for Ward Lock Educational
47 Marylebone Lane, London W1M 6AX
Made in Great Britain

CONTENTS

THE IMPORTANCE OF THINGS

Things you like and dislike — using lists of things to create atmosphere or to describe a place and time — what makes writing vivid?

This first book is primarily about things — the look of things, the sound of things, the smell of things, the taste of things, and the feel of things. And so the first poem is a poem in praise of things, and the different stuff they're made of. Most of the verses are rather like riddles: they don't tell you what they're about until the third line, though you may be able to guess from the first two.

STUFF

Lovers lie around in it
Broken glass is found in it
Grass
I like that stuff

Tuna fish get trapped in it
Legs come wrapped in it
Nylon
I like that stuff

Eskimos and tramps chew it
Madame Tussaud gave status to it
Wax
I like that stuff

Elephants get sprayed with it
Scotch is made with it
Water
I like that stuff

Clergy are dumbfounded by it
Bones are surrounded by it
Flesh
I like that stuff

Carpenters make cots of it
Undertakers use lots of it
Wood
I like that stuff

Cigarettes are lit by it
Pensioners get happy when they sit by it
Fire
I like that stuff

Dankworth's alto is made of it, most of it
Scoobdedoo is composed of it
Plastic
I like that stuff

Man-made fibres and raw materials
Old rolled gold and breakfast cereals
Platinum linoleum
I like that stuff

Skin on my hands
Hair on my head
Toenails on my feet
And linen on my bed

Well I like that stuff
Yes I like that stuff
The earth
Is made of earth
And I like that stuff

ADRIAN MITCHELL

Which of the stuff he mentions do *you* like best? Why? What other things do you think he ought to have mentioned? You might like to try writing a few extra verses of your own. If you find the rhyme too difficult to manage, write them without. It's better to say what you want to say than to say something else just because of the rhymes.

The next piece is part of a poem by Rupert Brooke. The poem is called *The Great Lover*; it's not about his girl-friends, but about the *things* he loves — sights, sounds, feelings, and even tastes and smells. Here's his list. As you read it, try to imagine each of the things he mentions.

These I have loved:
                    White plates and cups, clean-gleaming,
Ringed with blue lines; and feathery, faery dust;
Wet roofs, beneath the lamp-light; the strong crust
Of friendly bread; and many-tasting food;
Rainbows; and the blue bitter smoke of wood;
And radiant raindrops couching in cool flowers;
And flowers themselves, that sway through sunny hours,
Dreaming of moths that drink them under the moon;
Then, the cool kindliness of sheets, that soon
Smooth away trouble; and the rough male kiss
Of blankets; grainy wood; live hair that is
Shining and free; blue-massing clouds; the keen
Unpassioned beauty of a great machine;
The benison of hot water; furs to touch;
The good smell of old clothes; and others such —
The comfortable smell of friendly fingers,
Hair's fragrance, and the musty reek that lingers
About dead leaves and last year's ferns . . . .
                                        Dear names,
And thousand other throng to me! Royal flames;
Sweet water's dimpling laugh from tap or spring;
Holes in the ground; and voices that do sing;
Voices in laughter, too; and body's pain,
Soon turned to peace; and the deep-panting train;
Firm sands; the little dulling edge of foam
That browns and dwindles as the wave goes home;
And washen stones, gay for an hour; the cold
Graveness of iron; moist black earthen mould;
Sleep; and high places; footprints in the dew;
And oaks; and brown horse-chestnuts, glossy-new;
And new-peeled sticks; and shining pools on grass;
All these have been my loves.

Which of the things he mentions do you like most? Which did you find easiest to imagine? Is it easier to imagine 'the strong crust of friendly bread' or 'many-tasting food'? Why should this be so?

Why does Brooke describe sheets as 'cool and kindly'? What does he mean by the 'rough male kiss' of blankets? When he wrote about 'the deep-panting train' he was thinking, of course, of a steam train.

How would you describe the sound of a diesel locomotive standing in a station with its engine running?

Here is a girl's poem about the things she likes:

I like the patter of horses' feet as they gallop;
A cool wind on hot days;
Chip 'butties' when the chip man's been.
The feel of grass on my feet.
To see Infants' paintings; climbing trees.
Writing and sums.
To hear the rustling of trees; stroking my pets
    and tickling my hamsters underneath.
The sizzling of chips; smelling the clean sheets.
Making up games on my own.
Singing birds in the trees.
The ticking of a grandfather clock.
Sewing things.
Thinking up poems for Mom to read.
Smelling flowers and sweet things.
I like watching the clouds go by.
Walking in the sand in my bare feet.
I like the scent of new mown grass.
The whistle of the kettle.
I like watching Mom knitting and hearing the clatter
    of her needles.
I like swimming, and brushing my hair.

JENNY BATSFORD

Did you notice how Jenny has found things she likes for each of her senses? There are things to see, things to hear, things to smell, things to feel, and things to taste. Do you know what 'chip butties' are?

Now make your own list of things you like. If you want to, start with 'These I have loved:' or just 'I like'. There's no need to write it as a poem — and certainly don't try to make to make it rhyme, otherwise you'll find you're putting in some things just because they rhyme, and not because you really like them. Don't forget things that you like the taste, smell and feel of, as well as things you like the look and sound of. Concentrate on particular things, even if they seem small or trivial — they're often the most vivid. If you have time afterwards, you can make another list of things you *dislike* — 'These I have loathed'!

● Whenever people write about their childhood, they seem to remember the long sunny days of summer. In the next piece, from *Cider with Rosie*, Laurie Lee writes about the summers of his boyhood. In the last paragraph, you'll see that he too uses a list of things — the things he remembers from those summers.

We sat by the roadside and scooped the dust with our hands and made little piles in the gutters. Then we slid through the grass and lay on our backs and just stared at the empty sky. There was nothing to do. Nothing moved or happened, nothing happened at all except summer. Small heated winds blew over our faces, dandelion seeds floated by, burnt sap and roast nettles tingled our nostrils together with the dull rust smell of dry ground. The grass was June high and had come up with a rush, a massed entanglement of species, crested with flowers and spears of wild wheat, and coiled with clambering vetches, the whole of it humming with blundering bees and flickering with scarlet butterflies. Chewing grass on our backs, the grass scaffolding the sky, the summer was all we heard; cuckoos crossed distances on chains of cries, flies buzzed and choked in the ears, and the saw-toothed chatter of mowing-machines drifted on waves of air from the fields.

We moved. We went to the shop and bought sherbet and sucked it through sticks of liquorice. Sucked gently, the sherbet merely dusted the tongue; too hard, and you choked with sweet powders; or if you blew back through the tube the sherbet-bag burst and you disappeared in a blizzard of sugar. Sucking and blowing, coughing and weeping, we scuffled our way down the lane. We drank at the spring to clean our mouths, then threw water at each other and made rainbows. Mr Jones's pond was bubbling with life, and covered with great white lilies — they poured from their leaves like candle-fat, ran molten, then cooled on the water. Moorhens plopped, and dabchicks scooted, insects rowed and skated. New-hatched frogs hopped about like flies, lizards gulped in the grass. . . .

Summer was also the time of these: of sudden plenty, of slow hours and actions, of diamond haze and dust on the eyes, of the valley in post-vernal slumber; of burying birds out of seething corruption; of Mother sleeping heavily at noon; of jazzing wasps and dragonflies, haystooks and thistle-seeds, snows of white butterflies, skylarks' eggs, bee-orchids, and frantic ants; of wolf-cub parades, and boy scouts' bugles; of sweat running down the legs; of boiling potatoes on bramble fires, of flames glass-blue in the sun; of lying naked in the hill-cold stream; begging pennies for bottles of pop; of girls' bare arms and unripe cherries, green apples and liquid walnuts; of fights and falls and new-scabbed knees, sobbing pursuits and flights; of picnics high up in the crumbling quarries, of butter running like oil, of sunstroke, fever, and cucumber peel stuck cool to one's burning brow. All this, and the feeling that it would never end, that such days had come for ever, with the pump drying up and the water-butt crawling, and the chalk ground hard as the moon. All sights twice-brilliant and smells twice-sharp, all game-days twice as long. Double charged as we were, like the meadow ants, with the frenzy of the sun, we used up the light to its last violet drop, and even then couldn't go to bed.

Even if you don't live in the country, summer is a good time, when you can get out with your friends in the evenings, and you don't have to be cooped up indoors. Most of us have happy memories of the summer. Is there anything that Laurie Lee mentions that reminds you of your own summer memories?

Imagine the following, and describe two or three of them:

(a) The sound of a bee, wasp or large fly against the window-pane.
(b) The taste of sherbet, and the feel of it in your mouth.
(c) The feel of scooping dust or sand with your hands, and making piles of it.
(d) The sound of a bugle.
(e) The feel of 'lying naked in the hill-cold stream'.
(f) The feel of 'cucumber peel stuck cool to one's burning brow'. (What would it feel like, too, after it had been stuck on for some time?)

Have another look at the last paragraph of the Laurie Lee passage, and then make your own similar list of the things you associate with summer, beginning 'Summer was the time of these:...' If you prefer, you can do the same for Spring, Autumn or Winter.

● The next poem is about Autumn — again in the country, this time in Kent. This too is a sort of list, and if you imagine the things the writer mentions you should get a picture of the Kent countryside in the Autumn.

THE LOOKER-ON

... And ladders leaning against damson trees,
And idle spades beside old garden walls,
And broken sickles covered up in leaves,
And baskets wet with dew, waist deep in grass,
And spider webs across half-open gates ...
   And memory of a moon, a giant rolling,
And, brown in moon's noonday, prolific oaks,
Glint of moonsilver on their solid acorns ...
   And a fierce sun melting the fringed horizon,
Cold grass, hard apples fallen and forgotten,
And dew-logged thistledown ... and crackling beechmast,
And plump matt mushrooms — beggar's harvest — white
As chalk, bland as a nut, and pink to break ...
   And bonfire incense, and bracken gold as beech,
And bearded hedges, latest blackberries,
Half-ploughed stubble and dusty threshing yards,
And early nights, cloud multitudes on fire ...

Dry noons, drenched dawns, deep scents, bright stars, lost
    thoughts . . .
       And empty orchards and wide open fields,
And robin solos in deserted woods,
And chimney smoke, and starry candlelight,
And far-off fields, and distances like the past,
And mossy silence, and the scent of leisure,
And spider webs across half-open gates,
And broken sickles buried under leaves,
And idle spades beside old garden walls,
And ladders leaning against damson trees, . . .

FRANK KENDON

Whether a piece of writing is vivid or not depends partly on the writer and partly on the reader. For instance, if you don't know what a robin sounds like you won't find the 'robin solos' bit very easy to imagine. But the writer can help by making the things he mentions precise, and not too general or vague — for instance, 'A curled leaf spiralled down from the horse-chestnut tree' is easier to imagine (if you know what a horse-chestnut tree is!) and says as much as, 'It was Autumn, and although there was little wind the leaves were falling from the trees.' Which of the things in Frank Kendon's poem did you find most vivid? Can you see why? Which things did you find least vivid?

The Looker-On is really just another list of things — this time from a particular place and time — joined together by 'and's. You'll see that most lines begin with 'And', and the poem ends in the same way that it starts. There is no rhyme. Here is a similar poem, written by someone at school, about morning in a city:

. . . And rubbish piled against walls,
And people pausing to look in shop windows,
And milk bottles on a doorstep waiting to be taken in,
And the tinkle of a bell as a shop door is opened,
And footsteps on the pavement,
And the roaring of lorries as they speed by,
And the high-pitched whine of a milk cart as it lumbers by,

And a man coughing in the street,
And people pausing to look in shop windows,
And rubbish piled against walls, . . .

A. J. HYNARD

**Write your own poem like this, about a place and time you know
well. It needn't be about a place in the country, nor about Autumn
— nor, for that matter, about a city in Spring!**

THE THING ITSELF

Description of objects brought into the classroom — looking at
and describing animals — using the shape of a poem to show an
animal's movement.

Whenever you're writing a story, or a description, or a poem, it's most important to concentrate *hard* on the thing you're writing about. Never mind about clever writing, or being 'poetic', or impressing your teacher or friends: concentrate on the thing you're writing about, and do your best to get it right, so that, afterwards, you can say, 'That's exactly how it was.'

Ted Hughes, the poet, has this to say about it:

> . . . Imagine what you are writing about. See it and live it. Do not think it up laboriously, as if you were working out mental arithmetic. Just look at it, touch it, smell it, listen to it, turn yourself into it. When you do this, the words look after themselves, like magic. If you do this you do not have to bother about commas or full-stops or that sort of thing. You do not look at the words either. You keep your eyes, your ears, your nose, your taste, your touch, your whole being on the thing you are turning into words. The minute you flinch, and take your mind off this thing, and begin to look at the words and worry about them . . . then your worry goes into them and they set about killing each other. So you keep going as long as you can, then look back and see what you have written. After a bit of practice, and after telling yourself a few times that you do not care how other people have written about this thing, this is the way you find it; and after telling yourself you are going to use any old word that comes into your head so long as it seems right at the moment of writing it down, you will surprise yourself. You will read back through what you have written and you will get a shock. You will have captured a spirit, a creature.

Good writing is never something you can 'run off', no matter how good at English you may be. It requires hard concentration, harder than that required in other school activities. And that concentration must be, first and foremost, on the thing you are writing about.

If you're not very good at spelling or punctuation, you may be surprised that Ted Hughes says you don't have to bother about commas, full-stops or words. But the important thing while you're writing is to concentrate on what you're writing about. After all, if necessary, you can always go through it afterwards and put the spelling and punctuation right.

Of course, it's much easier to describe something when you've got the thing in front of you: you can keep on checking to make sure you've got it right. Here's what one boy wrote about a winged sycamore seed he was given in class:

A SYCAMORE SEED

He lies over my desk, a shrivelled brown object. But there is more to him than that. At first let us take the seed itself. It is roughly an oval shape, but it is very flat. At the bottom there is a flat thin short section where the stalk once attached itself. It seems to have an inner ring, which explains the layers that can be found on the stalk. This section comes sharply to two tiny points at the front. From here a strong ridge, like a backbone, runs over the top of the seed. Its main purpose seems to be to bind the seed together and to provide an extra strapping for the large wing. Actually the wing seems to have dropped slightly and this top connection has parted and the back of the seed is split on either side, showing white tissue. The rest of the back and undersurface is taken up by the joint of the larger wing. The main veins and connection come from the rear of the seed. The seed is mainly a darkish brown, giving way to a green tinge at the extreme top.

In this seed the veins are all broken but it is easy to see that they form the essential backbone for the wing. Naturally they converge and run along the top of the wing and branch off like tributaries, no doubt once used for food conveyance. The wing is grey with both white and blackish patches, though one side entirely lacks the black. It is torn and frayed at the edges and the centre lacks some pieces. It is extremely thin and brittle.

Now the wing is broken off and the seed opened. Inside there is a green kernel, unfortunately split. This is built in many layers, like a cabbage heart. It is cushioned by thick layers of white fluff, and these are so well fitted that it is difficult to see the brown innerside of the outer case. Around the inner kernel there is a final protective brown layer. I think now that the two splits on the outer shell were natural, for the shell opened easily along these edges.

If the wing itself is dropped, that is, without the seed, it flutters aimlessly to the floor. This suggests that the wing is set at a slight angle, which is indeed so, with the backbone uppermost, and when the seed falls, the air pressure on the underside of the wing drives it round and round, thus delaying its fall, and giving time for the wind to act. This indeed it must, for if the seed falls below the big tree, as the majority in fact do, it is doomed, for the mother tree chokes the life out of its little one. It can find little light, food, or moisture, and so growth is limited at the best.

What better means of seed transportation can one find? How very successful these seeds are. Their flight is extraordinarily good, and the seed construction is perfectly adapted to its needs. They need not fall far away, just out of the spread of the mother tree. And yet, out of all the thousands of seeds that fall, so few are destined to grow.

ROGER LINDLEY

Even if you hadn't been told, you would know that the boy who wrote this had the seed in front of him at the time. How?

The boy concentrates hard on the seed the whole time, though in the last paragraph and a half he thinks more generally about seeds and their place in the natural cycle. What else suggests that he is interested in Science and nature generally?

But you don't have to be an expert to describe something vividly. 'Just look at it, touch it, smell it, listen to it, turn yourself into it', as Ted Hughes says. That's what the boy who wrote this description of *A Dead Holly Leaf* has done — in fact, he seems to have tasted it too!

This dead holly leaf has been dead so long that it has turned into a kind of skeleton. You can see the veins clearly. It is a very light brown. In some places rotted remnants are still clinging to the skeleton. These are a greyish brown. These

patches break up the clearness of the leaf. It is very fragile, and just a little jerk will break it. It is so thin that you can feel your skin on both sides when you pick it up. The larger veins are divided between each other by hundreds of smaller veins. It looks very delapidated and dirty. It tastes of nothing in particular except earth and grass. It smells faintly of proper holly.

The leaf was fixed to the holly bush by a slender, light-brown twig. This tastes like the wood they use for making pencils.

It looks a very weird thing sitting on my book. It is about four inches long by two inches wide. It has holes all over the place, some large, others small. It is very light and extremely thin.

ANDREW JACKSON

Which of the details he mentions seems most vivid to you? Can you say why? The boy obviously wrote down these details as they occurred to him. Can you see any places where he might have done better to mention them in a different order?

Write your own description of something you can have in front of you while you are writing. It's best to choose something small, that you've never looked at closely before. A leaf, a small flower like a daisy, or even a small stone is quite a good thing to write about.

● **The next poem, by Theodore Roethke, is less scientific and much simpler, but even here he starts off by keeping his eye firmly on the field mouse he is writing about; it's almost as if he was looking at it while he was writing.**

THE MEADOW MOUSE

I

In a shoe box stuffed in an old nylon stocking
Sleeps the baby mouse I found in the meadow,
Where he trembled and shook beneath a stick
Till I caught him up by the tail and brought him in,

Cradled in my hand,
A little quaker, the whole body of him trembling,
His absurd whiskers sticking out like a cartoon-mouse,
His feet like small leaves,
Little lizard-feet,
Whitish and spread wide when he tried to struggle away,
Wriggling like a miniscule puppy.

Now he's eaten his three kinds of cheese and drunk from
    his bottle-cap watering-trough —
So much he just lies in one corner,
His tail curled under him, his belly big
As his head; his bat-like ears
Twitching, tilting towards the least sound.

Do I imagine he no longer trembles
When I come close to him?
He seems no longer to tremble.

        II
But this morning the shoe-box on the back porch is empty.
Where has he gone, my meadow mouse,
My thumb of a child that nuzzled in my palm? —
To run under the hawk's wing.
Under the eye of the great owl watching from the elm tree,
To live by courtesy of the shrike, the snake, the tom-cat.

I think of the nestling fallen into the deep grass,
The turtle gasping in the dusty rubble of the highway,
The paralytic stunned in the tub, and the water rising, —
All things innocent, hapless, foresaken.

THEODORE ROETHKE

The poem starts with a very vivid description of the mouse, and then, at the end, Theodore Roethke allows his thoughts about the mouse to develop so that they include all innocent creatures that suffer. Look at the description of the mouse. Which details sound particularly true? Roethke is not frightened of using unusual ideas

in his efforts to get the description right. What do you think he means by 'His feet like small leaves, Little lizard-feet'? Why is the mouse like the 'thumb of a child that nuzzled in my palm'?

Write about an animal (or bird, or even insect) you know well. If you are able to, write with the animal in front of you. If not, *imagine* that it is in front of you. Try to include precise details that will make it real to your reader. What sort of noise does it make? What is it like to handle? Has it got a smell?

● It's not easy to get an animal to stand still while you write about it, and, in any case, describing the way it moves is quite an important part of the description. In the next poem, D. H. Lawrence describes trying to chase a bat out of his room. His description is so vivid that it's almost as if he wrote the poem down at the time — though in this case he obviously couldn't have done! Notice the way he gets the movement of the bat — and himself — into the sound of the lines.

MAN AND BAT

When I went into my room, at mid-morning,
Say ten o'clock . . .
My room, a crash-box over that great stone rattle
The Via de' Bardi . . .

5 When I went into my room at mid-morning
Why? . . . a bird!

A bird
Flying round the room in insane circles.

In insane circles!
10 . . . A *bat!*

A disgusting bat
At mid-morning! . . .

Out! Go out!

24

Round and round and round
15 With a twitchy, nervous, intolerable flight,
And a neurasthenic lunge,
And an impure frenzy;
A bat, big as a swallow!

Out, out of my room!

20 The venetian shutters I push wide
To the free, calm upper air;
Loop back the curtains . . .

Now out, out from my room!

So to drive him out, flickering with my white handkerchief:
25   *Go!*
But he will not.

Round and round and round
In an impure haste,
Fumbling, a beast in air,
30 And stumbling, lunging and touching the walls, the bellwires
About my room!

Always refusing to go out into the air
Above that crash-gulf of the Via de' Bardi,
Yet blind with frenzy, with cluttered fear.

35 At last he swerved into the window bay,
But blew back, as if an incoming wind blew him in again.
A strong inrushing wind.

And round and round and round!
Blundering more insane, and leaping, in throbs, to clutch
40   at a corner,
At a wire, at a bell-rope:
On and on, watched relentless by me, round and round in
    my room,
Round and round and dithering with tiredness and haste and
45   increasing delirium

Flicker-splashing round my room.

I would not let him rest;
Not one instant cleave, cling like a blot with his breast
   to the wall
50 In an obscure corner.
Not an instant!

I flicked him on,
Trying to drive him through the window.

Again he swerved into the window bay
55 And I ran forward, to frighten him forth.
But he rose, and from a terror worse than me he flew past
   me
Back into my room, and round, round, round in my room
Clutch, cleave, stagger,
60 Dropping about the air
Getting tired.

Something seemed to blow him back from the window
Every time he swerved at it;
Back on a strange parabola, then round, round, dizzy in
65   my room.

He *could* not go out;
I also realized . . .

It was the light of day which he could not enter,
Any more than I could enter the white-hot door of a
70   blast-furnace.
He could not plunge into the daylight that streamed at the
   window.
It was asking too much of his nature.

Worse even than the hideous terror of me with my handker-
75   chief
Saying: *Out, go out!* . . .
Was the horror of white daylight in the window!

So I switched on the electric light, thinking: *Now*
The outside will seem brown . . .
80 But no.
The outside did not seem brown.
And he did not mind the yellow electric light.

Silent!
He was having a silent rest.
85 *But never!*
Not in my room.

Round and round and round
Near the ceiling as if in a web
Staggering;
90 Plunging, falling out of the web,
Broken in heaviness,
Lunging blindly,
Heavier;
And clutching, clutching for one second's pause,
95 Always, as if for one drop of rest,
One little drop.

And I!
Never, I say . . .
Go out!

100 Flying slower,
Seeming to stumble, to fall in air.
Blind-weary.

Yet never able to pass the whiteness of light into freedom . . .
A bird would have dashed through, come what might.

105 Fall, sink, lurch, and round and round
Flicker, flicker-heavy;
Even wings heavy:
And cleave in a high corner for a second, like a clot, also
     a prayer.

110 *But no.*
Out, you beast.

Till he fell in a corner, palpitating, spent.
And there, a clot, he squatted and looked at me.
With sticking-out, bead-berry eyes, black,
115 And improper derisive ears,
And shut wings,
And brown, furry body.

Brown, nut-brown, fine fur!
But it might as well have been hair on a spider; thing
120 With long, black-paper ears.

So, a dilemma!
He squatted there like something unclean.

No, he must not squat, nor hang, obscene, in my room!

Yet nothing on earth will give him courage to pass the
125   sweet fire of day.

What then?
Hit him and kill him and throw him away?

Nay,
I didn't create him.
130 Let the God that created him be responsible for his death . . .
Only, in the bright day, I will not have this clot in my room.

Let the God who is maker of bats watch with them in their
        unclean corners . . .
I admit a God in every crevice,
135 But not bats in my room;
Nor the God of bats, while the sun shines.

So out, out you brute! . . .
And he lunged, flight-heavy, away from me, sideways,
        a *sghembo!*
140 And round and round and round my room, a clot with wings
Impure even in weariness.

Wings dark skinny and flapping the air,
Lost their flicker.
Spent.

145 He fell again with a little thud
Near the curtain on the floor.
And there lay.

Ah, death, death,
You are no solution!
150 Bats must be bats.

Only life has a way out.
And the human soul is fated to wide-eyed responsibility
In life.

So I picked him up in a flannel jacket,
155 Well covered, lest he should bite me.
For I would have had to kill him if he'd bitten me, the
    impure one . . .
And he hardly stirred in my hand, muffled up.

Hastily, I shook him out of the window.

160 And away he went!
Fear craven in his tail.
Great haste, and straight, almost bird straight above the
    Via de' Bardi.
Above that crash-gulf of exploding whips,
165 Towards the Borgo San Jacopo.

And now, at evening, as he flickers over the river
Dipping with petty triumphant flight, and tittering over
    the sun's departure,
I believe he chirps, pipistrello, seeing me here on this
170   terrace writing:
There he sits, the long loud one!
But I am greater than he . . .
I escaped him . . .

D. H. LAWRENCE

Lawrence uses the length and shape of his lines, and their rhythm, to help suggest the movement of the man and bat, and the thoughts of the man about the bat. See if you can find lines where the rhythm and sound particularly suggest:

(a) The movement of the man.
(b) The movement of the bat in the room before it gets tired.
(c) The movement of the bat when it is tired.
(d) The bat's falling on the floor.
(e) The flight of the bat outside in the evening.

In lines 123 to 136 the man's thoughts seem to have two voices, as if he is talking to himself. What points of view do the different voices put, and how do the voices *sound* different? Is there anything to suggest that the man is frightened of the bat?

Now here is a much shorter poem by William Carlos Williams. It is about a cat. Read it very quietly, and take a little pause at the end of each line, and a slightly longer pause at the end of each verse. Imagine that the cat is moving when you are reading, and pausing when you are pausing, and you'll get an idea of the careful way it moves.

As the cat
climbed over
the top of

the jamcloset
first the right
forefoot

carefully
then the hind
stepped down

into the pit of
the empty
flowerpot.

Could you imagine the cat moving? Why is there such a big gap between 'forefoot' and 'carefully'?

You can write poems about other creatures in this way. Or you can space out your words in other ways to give an idea of how an animal moves. Here is another poem about a cat, this time by someone at school.

MOVEMENT, CATLIKE

Pit
        Pat
Pit   Pit
                    Pat
creep, stalk
                        Pounce
Run
        Scamper
                Dodge
    hide   watch   look   spot!
        creep, freeze
        creep, freeze
            R u n
                freeze
        pounce
                fight
        rip   claw
    tear   bite   KILL

    play   chew   chase
        'dab'   smell
        leave   run

            forget.

N. BOULTER

Now try writing your own poem about a creature moving. If you like, write about trying to get rid of a wasp, or a spider, in the way Lawrence writes about the bat, or write a poem like one of those about the cats, perhaps about some other animal. Don't make your poem rhyme; there are more important things to think of in a poem of this kind.

THINGS IN THEIR PLACES

Taking notes for description — shaping the notes into a more finished piece of writing — descriptive poems using vivid details — condensing, and concentrating on one detail — short poems putting two pictures together — Haiku.

Good description is largely a question of mentioning the right things. When you want to describe a scene it's therefore quite a good idea to jot down a list of the things you can see, hear, feel and smell (and sometimes taste). You can even list them under these headings if it helps you to remember. You'll find your list of things you can smell or feel is much shorter than your list of things you can hear or see. But don't be tempted to mention only the big things you can see: a small detail often tells you just as much — and is far more vivid.

● Wilfred Owen, a poet who was killed in the First World War, made one of his pre-war diary entries into a more formal poem:

FROM MY DIARY, JULY 1914

Leaves
    Murmuring by myriads in the shimmering trees.
Lives
    Wakening with wonder in the Pyrenees.
Birds
    Cheerily chirping in the early day.
Bards
    Singing of summer scything through the hay.
Bees
    Shaking the heavy dews from bloom and frond.
Boys
    Bursting the surface of the ebony pond.
Flashes
    Of swimmers carving thro' the sparkling cold.
Fleshes
    Gleaming with wetness to the morning gold.
A mead
    Bordered about with warbling water brooks.
A maid
    Laughing the love-laugh with me; proud of looks.
The heat
    Throbbing between the upland and the peak.
Her heart
    Quivering with passion to my pressed cheek.

Braiding
    Of floating flames across the mountain brow.
Brooding
    Of stillness; and a sighing of the bough.
Stirs
    Of leaflets in the gloom; soft petal-showers;
Stars
    Expanding with the starr'd nocturnal flowers.

You'll see the short lines are really just a list of things, while the longer lines that follow them say more about the things. The long lines rhyme in pairs — how do the short lines rhyme? Are there any lines that seem to you to be put in just to fit the rhyming scheme, rather than because of what they say?

After taking notes around the boiler room at his school, M. J. Randall made the notes into a poem that is rather like Wilfred Owen's:

THE CELLAR STEPS

A boiler,
    Murmuring with a consistent beat.
Cobwebs,
    Climbing down the dirty drainpipe.
Water,
    A black puddle, as ugly as the litter in it.
A workman,
    Whistling as the boiler is silenced.

        I turn round:

The sun,
    Giving the old roofs a golden glance.
Fish and chips,
    The smell waits over the old flint walls.
Laughing,

As people walk past on the other side of the wall.

I turn round again as

The workman
Puts his foot in the oily puddle.

Write your own poem like this, using short and long lines alternately. The short lines should be a list of things, and the long lines should say something more about those things, perhaps saying what they are doing. It's probably a good idea if you can take notes first.

● **Quite a lot of descriptive poems get their effect because of the vivid things — or images — they mention. Look at this well-known poem by T. S. Eliot:**

PRELUDE

The winter evening settles down
With smell of steaks in passageways.
Six o'clock.
The burnt-out ends of smoky days.
And now a gusty shower wraps
The grimy scraps
Of withered leaves about your feet
And newspapers from vacant lots;
The showers beat
On broken blinds and chimney-pots,
And at the corner of the street
A lonely cab-horse steams and stamps.
And then the lighting of the lamps.

Look at the things he mentions. There are things to see, things to hear, things to feel, things to smell — some of you may even find

something to taste in the second line! Find examples of each. With which sense would you notice 'Six o'clock'? Which idea in the poem do you find the most vivid? Why?

Douglas Dunn is famous for his vivid poems about Terry Street. Here is one of them, called *Late Night Walk down Terry Street*.

A policeman on a low-powered motorcycle stops.
His radio crackles, his helmet yellows.

Empty buses heading for the depot
Rush past the open end of Terry Street.

In their light, a man with a bike walking home,
Too drunk to ride it, turns into Terry Street.

Taxis swerve down Terry Street's shortcut,
Down uneven halls of Street Lighting Department yellow.

Into which now comes the man with the bike,
Struggling to keep on his legs.

The policeman waits under a gone-out streetlamp.
He stops the drunk, they talk, they laugh together.

I pass them then, beside dark, quiet houses,
In others mumbling sounds of entertainment;

Cathode-glows through curtains, faint latest tunes;
Creaking of bedsprings, lights going out.

It looks almost too easy! It's as if Douglas Dunn has just jotted down things as he saw them! But notice the way the last two lines tie the poem up.

Try writing a poem like this about *your* street or road. It's obviously best if you can write it looking out into the street, but, if you can't, do it from notes or memory. It needn't be at night-time; it could be early morning, or a Sunday.

If you prefer, write a poem like T. S. Eliot's *Prelude*. Make certain the things you mention are vivid — and don't forget the feel and smell of things.

● A description doesn't have to mention a lot of things to be vivid. Often a whole scene can be brought to life by one really good and vivid detail, as in this poem by William Carlos Williams:

BETWEEN WALLS

the back wings
of the

hospital where
nothing

will grow lie
cinders

in which shine
the broken

pieces of a green
bottle

In this poem, the poet is trying to present a vivid detail as simply as possible. In the next poem a boy at school has condensed the whole idea of Autumn into a picture of a wind-blown rose:

AUTUMN

The rain has stopped.
One solitary rose remains, drooping.
Its stalk is brown;
Its leaves are wet.

Raindrops cling in clusters
To the spiky thorns.
A cold wet wind blows,
And the white raindrops fall.

PHILIP WILLIAMSON

In some ways it is easier to make poems like these vivid. A small thing is usually easier to imagine than a big thing . In Philip's piece, it's difficult not to think that he has the rose in front of him as he writes it! Why are the raindrops 'white'?

Write your own short poem about something small that will make a whole scene vivid. If you like, make it the same shape as the poem 'Between Walls'.

● As Ezra Pound was watching the white faces of people coming up from the dark of the Paris Underground (the Metro) into the light of the street, he suddenly and vividly remembered something he had once seen before. He put the two ideas together into a short poem.

IN A STATION OF THE METRO

The apparition of these faces in the crowd;
Petals on a wet, black bough.

Why do you think the faces in the crowd made him think of 'Petals on a wet, black bough'? How are the two pictures similar?

Here are some poems written by people at school after reading the poem by Ezra Pound. Which do you like best? Why?

Chalk dust in the air;
A dry cold mist.

PETER MILNE

Stars twinkling in the night sky;
Broken glass under the midday sun.

JAMES MACKAY

A flash of blank, puzzled looks;
Lightning, striking a tumbledown shack.

GRAHAM HALSEY

Write some of these two-line poems of your own, comparing two different pictures — one in each line. See how vivid you can make them.

● Here is a translation of a Japanese poem. This kind of poem is called a *Haiku*. It has three lines, and usually three ideas, related in a special way.

On a bare branch
A rook rests:
Autumn dusk.

MATSUO BASHŌ

If you look again at the poem you will notice that in each of the first two lines a particular thing is mentioned, making a vivid picture. The last line seems to give the poem its title. Sometimes a haiku is built the other way round:

Winter rain:
A farmhouse piled with firewood,
A light in the window.

NOZAWA BONCHŌ

In the original Japanese, a Haiku has seventeen syllables — five in the first line, seven in the second, and five in the third. Here's a haiku written in English by an Englishman, in which he's obeyed the syllable rules:

5   Wind lifts suddenly —
7   Balloon lurches from small hand
5   Clutching nothing now.

NEIL FERGUSON

Try writing a Haiku of your own. You can obey the syllable rules if you like, but there's no need to. It's more important to mention the right things in each line, so that over-all they make a vivid picture. Have another look through the examples before you start.

LOOKING AND SEEING

Colours — the way a painter looks at a scene — colour and atmosphere — the way the eye moves — colour and the vivid detail.

Have you ever thought what it would be like to be blind? If you had to make a list of the seven sights you've most liked seeing, what would they be? Try writing a description of one of them. How would your description be different if you were trying to explain the sight to a person who had been blind from birth?

How would you describe colours to a blind man? You might begin by saying red was a bright, loud colour, which stands out and which makes people think of fire, heat, blood and anger. How would you describe green, blue, yellow or orange? Can you link colours with sounds, or feelings, or smells?

The boys who wrote the next two poems have given some of the things they associate with different colours.

Red — a bike propped against a wall; blood trickling down a finger.
Blue — the sky; the sea on a clear day; a boat on its way to port.
Black — a sleek cat walking through the grass; the night, cold and unfriendly.
Green — a field, unhedged, rolling into the distance; broken bottles by the seaside.
Yellow — the sun; a flower blooming among the grass.
Brown — a bird soaring above in the sky; mud, slushy and dirty.
White — clouds, slowly drifting across the sky; a wall untouched and new; a yacht with all sails set.

B. J. ALDWELL

Black — My pen, uniform, dullness, fear;
        My cat, flowing hairs, blindness.
Grey — Tarmac, clouds, uncertainty;
        Hollowness, machinery, metals.
White — Cleanness, paper, light;
        Shine, bones, home bedrooms.
Red — Blood, hatred, fear, death;
        Cars, speed, poisons.

Green — Grass, trees, freedom, joy;
          Lions, beauty, care, love.
Blue — Sky, sea, thought, emptiness;
          Longing, sight.

HAMID TOOFANIAN

Try writing your own poem about colours and what you associate them with, or, if you prefer, choose your favourite colour and write about that.

● ***The Horse's Mouth* is a book about a painter, and it is written from the painter's point of view. Here is a description of the River Thames, which the painter obviously is thinking of painting:**

On the Surrey side the fire was dead. Clouds all in blue and blue-in-soot. Blue-black smoke drifting up like smoky candles, and a blue sky as blue as blue spectacles with long pieces of sooty cobwebs floating high up. Stars coming through like needle points; green-blue, neon blue; and the river pouring quietly along, as bright as ink out of a bottle. All below as flat as melted iron, on three levels; first Greenbank hard; then a step down to the river, and a step up to the towpath; then away to the edge of the plate. A flat earth. A few knobs of trees and houses popping up to make it flatter. And all above on one curve about ten thousand feet high. Sweet as the inside of a dish cover. The cobwebs hung on nothing in the middle, to make it hollower.

As simple as Euclid. Grand as the field of glory. Almost a picture ready-made, I said. There's more than a sketch there — it's got some composition. And my fingers ached to do it.

We'd got to the railing next the motor factory and Barberry Creek. It was half-tide, and there were three barges cock-eye on the serge-blue mud. So that they tilted on the ramp. Like stranded whales with their waists in the water. And a brazier full of orange-hot coke making a hay-green high light on their snouts. Two men and a boy moving about throwing shadows fifty yards long, right to our feet. Carrying long tar-brushes, like brooms.

It made my mouth water. I could have eaten those personal chunks of barges and that sweet individual flank of mud.

JOYCE CARY

Read the passage again, looking carefully at the way the scenes are described. What kind of paintings do you think the artist paints? What would they be like?

There are really two pictures here: the first is described in the first two paragraphs, and the second in the last two. What would the first picture be like when painted by the artist? What would be the most impressive colour? How would the colour of the second painting be different?

Describe the view from your window, or some other scene that you know well, as if you were an artist who was going to paint it. Take careful note of colour and shape. It's obviously best if you can have the scene in front of you while you are writing, as if you were sketching it, but if you can't, imagine that you're actually there.

● Thomas Carlyle begins his poem *To-day* with the words:

So here hath been dawning
Another blue day:
Think, wilt thou let it
Slip useless away?

What do you think he means by saying that the day is 'blue'? What might someone mean by a 'grey day', a 'brown day', or a 'yellow day'?

Sometimes, a day, or a particular scene, seems to have one over-all colour, even when individual things are different colours. Painters often try to bring out this over-all colour, putting a little bit of it into all the paints they use. If you look back at the passage from *The Horse's Mouth*, and at the pictures, you will see examples.

What are the main colours in each of these? Poets and writers sometimes try to do the same thing. Here is a poem about the Thames, 'painted' in one colour:

EMBANKMENT BEFORE SNOW

A zinc afternoon. The barges black,
And black the funnels of tugs nosing
Phlegm-coloured waves slap-slapping
Stone wharves. A smell of sacking
And soot. Grey chimneys, and statues
Grey with cold, and grey lifebelts.

ALAN ROSS

What colour does Alan Ross see the Thames as? What time of year do you think it is in his poem?

Write your own description of a day or scene which strikes you as being 'blue', 'yellow', 'green', 'brown' or 'grey'. Try to bring out the colour you've chosen. If you're feeling ambitious, you may prefer to write about a day or scene that's some other colour — red, violet, or even purple!

● What is the difference between 'seeing' something and 'looking at' something? Pick some small thing on the wall in front of you, and stare at it. How far to the left and right can you *see* without moving your eyes? Move your hands to the left and right of your head to find out. It's surprising how wide a space you can *see* when you're only *looking at* one small detail. Try looking at the whole room at once. Is it possible?

When you go into a room, your eye moves from one small spot to another, taking in some things and missing others. Can you remember the first thing you looked at when you came into the room you're in now? Your teacher? The chair you were heading for? The blackboard?

This is why it's best to describe a scene by mentioning small details — your imagination works in much the same way as your eye. Here is another poem by William Carlos Williams:

THE RED WHEELBARROW

so much depends
upon

a red wheel
barrow

glazed with rain
water

beside the white
chickens

The colours are very important in helping us to picture this. If you were to change the colours of the wheelbarrow and the chickens it would be quite a different picture! Look back at the poem and you will see that the colour is important there, too.

Look at a row of books on a shelf. Which book does your eye catch on first? You'll find that it is often the colour of something that makes you pick on it.

Write a poem which describes a scene by mentioning a coloured detail which caught your eye. If you like, make it the same shape as *The Red Wheelbarrow*, starting
so much depends
on

LISTENING AND HEARING

Sounds you like — words that make the sounds themselves — sounds of times and places — noisy places: fairgrounds, railway stations, football matches.

NOISE

I like noise.
The whoop of a boy, the thud of a hoof,
The rattle of rain on a galvanized roof,
The hubbub of traffic, the roar of a train,
The throb of machinery numbing the brain,
The switching of wires in an overhead tram,
The rush of the wind, a door on the slam,
The boom of the thunder, the crash of the waves,
The din of a river that races and raves,
The crack of a rifle, the clank of a pail,
The strident tattoo of a swift-slapping sail —
From any old sound that the silence destroys
Arises a gamut of soul-stirring joys.
I like noise.

JESSIE POPE

Try to imagine the sounds that Jessie Pope mentions. Which do you find the easiest to imagine? A metal pail 'clanks' when you put it down. What sort of noise does it make when you are carrying it? What sort of noise does a fast-running river make?

If your school's near a railway, you may be able to hear the trains from your classroom. Describe the noise made by

   (a) A heavy diesel locomotive
   (b) A passenger train
   (c) A goods train shunting.

How does the sound of a train change when it goes under a bridge or into a tunnel?

Listen to the rhythm of a train and try to fit words to it — you can use words like 'bacon-and-eggs', 'liver-and-bacon' or 'bread-and-butter', or invent your own. Try putting them together to make a poem.

ALL SOUNDS HAVE BEEN AS MUSIC

All sounds have been as music to my listening:
  Pacific lamentations of slow bells,
The crunch of boots on blue snow rosy-glistening,
  Shuffle of autumn leaves; and all farewells:

Bugles that sadden all the evening air,
  And country bells clamouring their last appeals
Before the music of the evening prayer;
  Bridges, sonorous under carriage wheels.

Gurgles of sluicing surge through hollow rocks,
  The gluttonous lapping of the waves on weeds,
Whisper of grasses; the myriad-tinkling flocks,
  The warbling drawls of flutes and shepherds' reeds.

Thrilling of throstles in the clear blue dawn,
  Bees fumbling and fuming over the sainfoin-fields.

WILFRED OWEN

In this poem Wilfred Owen has listed some of the sounds he likes.
If you read it aloud, you'll notice that the sound of the words he uses
in the poem often give some idea of the sounds he is describing. For
instance, he uses long words ('pacific lamentations') to bring out the
slow, peaceful sadness of the bells in line 2, 'sloshy' words ('gurgles',
'sluicing', 'gluttonous', and 'lapping') to describe the water, 'humming' words for the bees, and so on. Which words fit the sounds
they describe best, do you think? How would *you* describe the sound
of a bugle? Would you call it a sad sound?

There are three different sounds of bells in the poem — the slow,
sad bells in line 2, the country bells in line 6, and the sheep-bells in
line 11 — and they all sound different. Do you have any bells in or
near your school, or at home? What sort of noise do they make?

Describe the sound of a telephone bell, or a hand-bell, or Big Ben

Make a list of the sounds *you* like. Try to give some idea of what they sound like, but you needn't do it in the same way that Wilfred Owen does unless you want to.

● As you can see in Wilfred Owen's poem, one way of describing noises is to use words that make a similar sound to the noise you're describing. Quite a lot of words do this — 'crunch', 'shuffle', 'gurgles', 'whisper' and 'warbling' are all good examples from the poem, and no doubt you can think of plenty more. Or you can even invent your own, as Alastair Reid does:

SOUNDS

PLOO
is breaking your shoelace.

MRRAAOWL
is what cats really say.

TRIS-TRAS
is scissors cutting paper.

KINCLUNK
is a car going over a manhole cover.

PHLOOPH
is sitting suddenly on a cushion.

CROOMB
is what pigeons murmur to themselves.

NYO-NYO
is speaking with your mouth full.

HARROWOLLOWORRAH
is yawning.

PALOOP
is the tap dripping in the bath.

RAM TAM GEE PICKAGEE
is feeling good.

Now invent some of your own. Here are some more examples by someone at school, to help you:

PHYT — Grandfather's lighter
KALIKALIKALIKALIK — Freewheeling on my bicycle
NIN NIN NIN NIN NIN NIN NIN NIN — The S.R.
   Electric train waiting to move off
KRISH KRISH KRISH — Me eating crisps

M. D. FEAVER

● **In this poem by Norman Nicholson, we read about three kinds of mornings and their sounds:**

WEATHER EAR

Lying in bed in the dark, I hear the bray
Of the furnace hooter rasping the slates, and say:
'The wind will be in the east, and frost on the nose, today.'

Or when, in the still, small, conscience hours, I hear
The market clock-bell clacking close to my ear:
'A north-west wind from the fell, and the sky-light swilled
                      and clear.'

But now when the roofs are sulky as the dead,
With a snuffle and sniff in the gullies, a drip on the lead:
'No wind at all, and the street stone-deaf with a cold in the
                      head.'

NORMAN NICHOLSON

In what part of the country do you think this poem is set? What do *you* hear in the mornings when you are at home and lying in bed? Do you hear other people getting up and going to work, or are you the first up? Do you need to be woken up in the morning? What does the person who wakes you up do and say?

Can you tell what sort of weather it is by the sound when you're still in bed? What does a foggy day sound like? What does a sunny day, or a wet day or a snowy day sound like?

In his play *Under Milk Wood*, Dylan Thomas describes the morning sounds of a small Welsh village:

There's the clip clop of horses on the sun honeyed cobbles of the humming streets, hammering of horseshoes, gobble quack and cackle, tomtit twitter from the bird-ounced boughs, braying on Donkey Down. Bread is baking, pigs are grunting, chop goes the butcher, milk-churns bell, tills ring, sheep cough, dogs shout, saws sing. Oh, the Spring whinny and morning moo from the clog dancing farms, the gulls' gab and rabble on the boat-bobbing river and sea and the cockles bubbling in the sand, scamper of sanderlings, curlew cry, crow caw, pigeon coo, clock strike, bull bellow, and the ragged gabble of the bear garden school as the women scratch and babble in Mrs Organ Morgan's general shop where everything is sold: custard, buckets, henna, rat-traps, shrimp-nets, sugar, stamps, confetti, paraffin, hatchets, whistles.

As in Wilfred Owen's '*All Sounds Have Been as Music*', Dylan Thomas's description uses words not only for their meaning, but for their sound and rhythm, in order to give the impression of the noisy bustle of the village — and obviously he's exaggerated his description to increase the impression. But though there's plenty of noise, there's no mention of motor traffic; so why does he describe the streets as 'humming'?

Now here's a description of the sounds heard from an open classroom window, in the middle of a city:

The gentle purr of the engine of a car, and the whooshing of the tyres on the wet road. The beep of a horn, the acceleration of a car, as the noise of the engine steadily gets higher. Silence. The sound of footsteps. High-heeled shoes tapping a regular beat on the paving stones. A car changes down a gear, and then another changes up. A shop door is opened with the 'ting' of a bell, and then shut again with the rattle of loose glass. The church bell rings its solitary note again and again, only to be drowned by the hollow roaring of a lorry's engine. Footsteps. The chirping of birds, resting on some building. The chimes go on. The slower footsteps of a person walking by.

Several cars go by. All of them seem to be changing gear. Again the whooshing shooshing sound of tyres on the tarmac. The strident beep of a car horn. An old milk cart starts off and rumbles into the distance. The tinkle of a bicycle bell and the splash of a bike in a puddle. I hear two voices outside. Men's voices. They have stopped. The on-off jerky sound of a British-Leyland bus as it twists its way through the street.

Silence as the windows are closed.

J. A. R. HARMS

How can you tell this was actually written at the time? Look at the way the various sounds are described. What detail seems most vivid to you? How is this description different from the Dylan Thomas piece, in the way it's written as well as in what it's about?

Listen carefully to the sounds you can hear from your class-room, and write your own description of them.

● It's difficult to imagine a railway station, or a school, or a football match, without imagining the noise they make. Here's a poem about a fairground by John Arlott:

BACK TO THE FAIR

Tonight, a cloud-rimmed flowering of the air
Has made a halo round the Autumn Fair —
That teeming, cluttered, music-churning dream
Where shrieking sirens flaunt their plumes of steam:
Crescendo symphony of penny joys
With counterpoint on counterpoint of noise —
The thwack of balls against the ninepin sheet,
The crunch of cinders under shuffled feet,
The power-impelling engine's rhythmic choke,
The bell that answers swaggered mallet's stroke,
The crang of shots that rake the rifle-range,
The chinking undertone of copper change.

The crowd is thickest where the switch-back races,
With castinetting wheels, the blur of faces,
The rushing round the bends to overtop
The heart-arresting, stomach-stealing drop:
There, organ-throned on high, the chip-faced gods
Still give their little, haughty, clockwork nods —
The hurdy-gurdy, steam-pulsed music stammers
With plinking of their rounded metal hammers.

The sparky hissing of the naphtha flares
Still haunts the thoughts of all my Autumn Fairs:
'The Greatest, Finest Fun Fair In The Land.'

My coppers tightly clenched in sweaty hand,
There's colour here, and only colour counts:
Those red-lipped stallions are my chosen mounts:
To saddle then, with fancied Cossack spring,
And, knees to flanks and hands to reins, I cling,
While, breathless, up and down and round and round
My painted steed careers in full-stretch bound.
I look around in dizzy horseman's pride
And scorn those earth-bound crowds who do not ride.
The man who nightly serves the roundabout —
A plimsoll-shod and shabby gipsy lout,
In shoddy, wasp-waist, double-breasted coat,
A greasy, near-silk muffler at his throat,
Whose baggy trousers mask a tiger's stride —
Appears like magic by my stirrup's side.
He grins and asks me for my 'tuppence, please,'
Then swings away with reckless, lounging ease,
And calmly counts his takings as he moves
Unscathed amidst that race of threshing hooves.

Fairs may have changed in some ways since this poem was written
— they now have electric light instead of naphtha flares, and diesel
generators instead of steam engines — but otherwise they are
much the same. What sounds in this poem do you like best? What
sounds would you hear at a modern fairground?

Imagine the sounds of the following, and describe two or three of
them:

   (a) An electric pin-table — one of those that flash numbers as
       the ball finds its way among the springs and flippers to the
       hole at the bottom.
   (b) A Hoop-La Stall — what noise does the hoop make as it
       falls?
   (c) A foot treading on an empty matchbox.
   (d) Dodg'ems — all of the sounds, not just the bump!
   (e) A coin falling on the floor.

Now write your own description of a fairground. If you prefer,
you could describe some other noisy scene, a railway station, or a
football match. But whatever you write about, think hard about the
sounds, and try to get them *right* in your description.

THE SENSE OF SMELL

Smells you like and dislike — interesting mixtures of smells — smells of places — smells and memories.

When we describe things, we usually say what they look like, and sometimes what they sound like, but we don't often mention what they taste like, what they smell like, or what they feel like to our sense of touch. Here is a poem about the smell of things. 'Gramarye' is a kind of magic, and 'Balsam' is pine resin. 'Camphor' is what moth balls are made of.

SMELLS

Why is it that the poets tell
So little of the sense of smell?
These are the odours I love well:

The smell of coffee freshly ground;
Of rich plum pudding, holly crowned;
Or onions fried and deeply browned.

The fragrance of a fumy pipe;
The smell of apples, newly ripe;
And printers' ink on leaden type.

Woods by moonlight in September
Breathe most sweet; and I remember
Many a smoky camp-fire ember.

Camphor, turpentine, and tea,
The balsam of a Christmas tree,
These are whiffs of gramarye . . .
A SHIP SMELLS BEST OF ALL TO ME!

CHRISTOPHER MORLEY

Try to imagine the smells he mentions, and describe two or three of them. It's very difficult to describe smells, even when you can imagine them, but try. It's sometimes helpful to think of smells in terms of colour (a green smell, or a brown smell), or taste (a sweet smell, a sour smell), or even touch (a sharp smell, a warm smell). See if you can find your own way of describing them.

What *does* a ship smell like? Tar and rope and seaweed? Or does it depend on what sort of ship it is? Imagine the smell of the following, and carefully describe one of them:

(a) a fishing boat
(b) a cross-Channel ferry
(c) a motor boat
(d) an aeroplane
(e) a car or bus.

Now make your own list of smells you like. Try to give some idea what sort of smell each is.

If you've time, you could make a similar list of smells you *don't* like.

● Although smells are very difficult to describe, it's well worth the effort. If you can make someone imagine the smell of something, it's not difficult for them to imagine the rest. Think of the smell of digging as you read the next poem.

DIGGING

To-day I think
Only with scents, — scents dead leaves yield,
And bracken, and wild carrot's seed,
And the square mustard field;

Odours that rise
When the spade wounds the root of tree,
Rose, currant, raspberry, or goutweed,
Rhubarb or celery;

The smoke's smell, too,
Flowing from where a bonfire burns
The dead, the waste, the dangerous,
And all to sweetness turns.

It is enough
To smell, to crumble the dark earth,
While the robin sings over again
Sad songs of Autumn mirth.

EDWARD THOMAS

Of course, you may find this difficult to imagine if you haven't done much digging. The smell depends, too, on whether you're digging in gravelly soil, or fine loam, or clay. And, as the poem says, the plants and roots you're digging through make a difference — some roots, like mint, or bindweed, have quite a strong smell.

Incidentally, what noise does a person make when he's digging or shovelling? It's not only pushing the spade in that makes the noise. You may need to act this out to get it right.

Well, even if you couldn't imagine the smell of digging, you should be able to cope with some of these next subjects. Describe the smell of one or two of them. Most of them are really a mixture of several different smells. See if you can work out what they are.

(a) A Greengrocer's Shop.
(b) A Hardware Shop.
(c) A Doctor's or Dentist's Surgery.
(d) School.
(e) Dustbins.

● The next two pieces are both about the smells of the seaside. The first is from Dylan Thomas's *Holiday Memory* of Swansea.

I remember the smell of sea and seaweed, wet flesh, wet hair, wet bathing-dresses, the warm smell as of a rabbity field after rain, the smell of pop and splashed sunshades and toffee, the stable-and-straw smell of hot, tossed, tumbled, dug, and trodden sand, the swill-and-gaslamp smell of Saturday night, though the sun shone strong, from the bellying beer-tents, the smell of the vinegar on shelled cockles, winkle-smell, shrimp-smell, the dripping-oily back-street winter-smell of chips in newspapers, the smell of ships from the sun-dazed docks round the corner of the sand-hills, the smell of the known and paddled-in sea . . .

Some of the ideas here need careful thinking about. Why, for instance, is the 'hot, tossed, tumbled, dug, and trodden sand' described as having a 'stable-and-straw' smell? Why is the smell of chips in newspapers a 'winter-smell'? Why do the beer-tents have the 'swill-and-gaslamp smell of Saturday night'?

In the next piece, John Betjeman remembers the holidays he spent in Cornwall as a boy. Here is a whole day of smells, starting with the early morning smell of bacon and finishing back in bed with the 'laundriness of sheets'.

Nose! Smell again the early morning smells:
Congealing bacon and my father's pipe;
The after-breakfast freshness out of doors
Where sun had dried the heavy dew and freed
Acres of thyme to scent the links and lawns;
The rotten apples on our shady path
Where blowflies settled upon squashy heaps,
Intent and gorging; at the garden gate
Reek of Solignum on the wooden fence;
Mint round the spring, and fennel in the lane,
And honey-suckle wafted from the hedge;
The Lynams' cess-pool like a body-blow;
Then, clean, medicinal and cold — the sea.

'Breathe in the ozone, John. It's iodine.'
But which is iodine and which is drains?
Salt and hot sun on rubber water-wings . . .
Home to the luncheon smell of Irish stew
And washing-up stench from the kitchen sink
Because the sump is blocked. The afternoons
Brought coconut smell of gorse; at Mably's farm
Sweet scent of drying cowdung; then the moist
Exhaling of the earth in Shilla woods —
First earth encountered after days of sand.
Evening brought back the gummy smell of toys
And fishy stink of glue and Stickphast paste,
And sleep inside the laundriness of sheets.

This is in many ways an easier piece to understand, if you can imagine the smells of the things he mentions. Certainly pipe-smoke, rotten apples and Solignum (a kind of Creosote) are easy enough.

Have you ever held your breath to avoid smelling something unpleasant? What happens when you *suddenly* come on an un-

pleasant smell? Can you see why the sewage smell of the Lynams'
cess-pool might be like a body-blow?

Now try to describe the smell of three or four of the following:

(a) A towel that is damp after being used by someone who has
    been swimming in the sea or in a swimming bath.
(b) Sand, especially sand at the sea-side.
(c) A damp newspaper — damp with water, not vinegar!
(d) Beer — the smell, not the taste!
(e) Fish and chips. (This *could* be too easy: try to say something
    new about the smell.)
(f) Bacon cooking.
(g) The smell of washing-up water in a blocked drain.

The last line but one mentions the 'fishy stink of glue and Stickphast paste'. Modern adhesives also have interesting smells. Think
of Bostik, Copydex, Seccotine, ordinary white paste, gum, Polycell
wallpaper paste, polystyrene cement, and the hard white Gripfix
that smells of almonds. Describe some of them.

Both of the pieces you've read are are really just lists of smells
to do with the seaside. Make your own list of smells from a particular time or place — it needn't necessarily be the seaside; think of a
place of your own. You may find it a help to begin with 'I remember
the smell of . . .', like Dylan Thomas, or, if you prefer, go through a
whole day's smells, as John Betjeman does. Make sure they are
accurately described, and easy to imagine.

●   The next two pieces are about the way a smell can bring back an
experience from the past and make it come alive again. First, here
is an extract from *Coming Up for Air*, by George Orwell.
Notice the way the story moves from the present (walking down
the Strand) to the past (in the church at Lower Binfield).

When I got down near Charing Cross the boys were yelling
a later edition of the evening papers. There was some more
drivel about the murder. LEGS. FAMOUS SURGEON'S
STATEMENT. Then another poster caught my eye: KING
ZOG'S WEDDING POSTPONED. King Zog! What a name!
It's next door to impossible to believe a chap with a name
like that isn't a jet-black Negro.

But just at that moment a queer thing happened. King
Zog's name — but I suppose, as I'd already seen the name
several times that day, it was mixed up with some sound in

the traffic or the smell of horse-dung or something — had started memories in me.

The past is a curious thing. It's with you all the time, I suppose an hour never passes without your thinking of things that happened ten or twenty years ago, and yet most of the time it's got no reality, it's just a set of facts you've learned, like a lot of stuff in a history book. Then some chance sight or sound or smell, especially smell, sets you going, and the past doesn't merely come back to you, you're actually in the past. It was like that at this moment.

I was back in the parish church at Lower Binfield, and it was thirty-eight years ago. To outward appearances, I suppose, I was still walking down the Strand, fat and forty-five, with false teeth and a bowler hat, but inside me I was Georgie Bowling, aged seven, younger son of Samuel Bowling, corn and seed merchant, of 57 High Street, Lower Binfield. And it was Sunday morning, and I could smell the church. How I could smell it! You know the smell churches have, a peculiar, dank, dusty, decaying, sweetish sort of smell. There's a touch of candle-grease in it, and perhaps a whiff of incense and a suspicion of mice, and on Sunday mornings it's a bit overlaid by yellow soap and serge dresses, but predominantly it's that sweet, dusty, musty smell that's like the smell of death and life mixed up together. It's powdered corpses, really.

Can you imagine the smell of a church? Do you think the description in the passage is a good one?

In the next poem, by Louis MacNeice, a man is washing his hands when the smell of the soap suddenly reminds him of the previous time he smelt it, when he was a boy of eight staying at a big house with 'a stuffed black dog in the hall', where he played croquet.

SOAP SUDS

This brand of soap has the same smell as once in the big
House he visited when he was eight: the walls of the bathroom open

To reveal a lawn where a great yellow ball rolls back through
    a hoop
To rest at the head of a mallet held in the hands of a child.

And these were the joys of that house: a tower with a
    telescope;
Two great faded globes, one of the earth, one of the stars;
A stuffed black dog in the hall; a walled garden with bees;
A rabbit warren; a rockery; a vine under glass; the sea.

To which he has now returned. The day of course is fine
And a grown-up voice cries Play! The mallet slowly swings,
Then crack, a great gong booms from the dog-dark hall and
    the ball
Skims forward through the hoop and then through the next
    and then

Through hoops where no hoops were and each dissolves in
    turn
And the grass has grown head-high and an angry voice cries
    Play!
But the ball is lost and the mallet slipped long since from the
    hands
Under the running tap that are not the hands of a child.

    You'll notice that this is described a bit like a 'flashback' in a film —
'the walls of the bathroom open / To reveal' a game of croquet.
This game of croquet is speeded up like a dream to show the passage
of time and the return to the present day and 'the hands / Under
the running tap that are not the hands of a child.'

    Look at his list of 'the joys of that house' in the second verse. Are
these the kind of things a child would remember? Can you make a
list of the 'joys' of a place you visited when you were small?

    Have you ever been reminded of a previous time and place by
a smell? Write about it, making clear what the smell was, and what
it took you back to.

FOOD AND THE SENSE OF TASTE

Food you like; your favourite meal — describing the taste of things — advertisements for food — describing something you're eating at the time — food and drink for different occasions — recipes and instructions — Leopold Bloom preparing breakfast — the importance of the feel and texture of food.

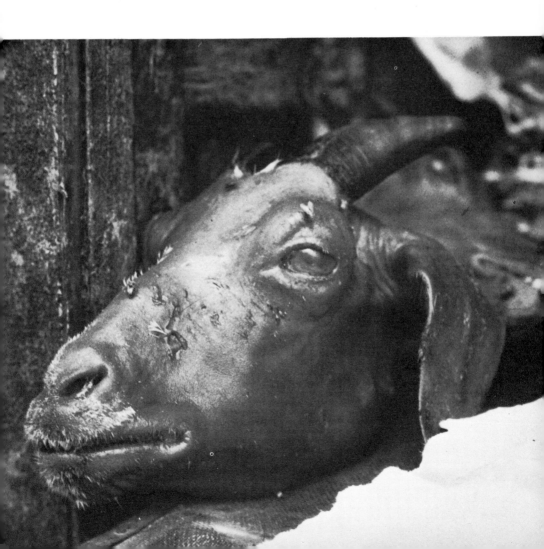

Our taste buds can only detect whether a thing is salt, sour, bitter or sweet. All the more subtle 'tastes' are in fact detected by our sense of smell. That is why we can't 'taste' when we have a cold, and why it's a help to hold the nose when taking an unpleasant medicine. Our sense of touch, too, helps us to enjoy food: with it we can tell whether food is crisp or smooth, hot or cold, and so on.

Since eating's such a popular activity, it's surprising that there aren't *more* poems in praise of food, like this Pygmy Song:

If you wish to walk for long in the forest
And to feel your heart strong,
Your breast swell sturdily,
And your legs run quickly,
Friend, grill on charcoal,
On the red coals of a burning fire,
The *won* with the cruel teeth,
The carp with a thousand colours
And the delicate firm flesh.

If you wish for calm sleep
To come softly and close your eyelids,
For joyful dreams, messengers from the dead,
To run and hunt at happy hunting,
The friendly place, where in the dark forest
The quick boar crouches near the stream,
And in the clearing among the peppermints
The fast antelope pricks up his ears,
Friend, in the leaves with which you are surrounded,
Friend, bake the *ngol*.

But if you wish for your heart
To be glad without regret,
For your belly, sated and full,
To say: 'Oh! Oh! that's enough!
Oh! Oh! I have eaten well!'
If you wish that your swollen belly
Should resist the finger that gladly presses it,
And sound under your hand like a stretched tom-tom,

A tom-tom of skin stretched to the utmost,
If you wish that your belly should sing a glad song,
Friend, take a *mpoi*, friend, eat a *mpoi*.

The first two verses are about foods that do you good, but the last verse is about something you can eat for sheer enjoyment, for the pleasure of feeling well-fed. Have you ever felt like this? How would you describe the feeling?

Perhaps you can guess what the *won*, the *ngol* and the *mpoi* are like. But in case you can't, think of your favourite foods and try to compile your perfect menu. What do you like about each item? Look at the following poem, written by a boy at school, and see how he has tried to give an idea of what each course is like.

FOOD

Two dry Tio Pepe
Refined liquid gold caresses the lips,
Infuses through the blanched almond teeth,
And subtly stimulates the palate.

Canelloni
Dark, firm, substantial offerings
Lie in a dish of silken brown,
Steeped in a sauce so rich and red.
Black burns — mince is minute —
Pancakes look like lunar surface.

Scallopine di Vitello alla Marsala
A picturesque title heralds
Grassy meads of veal and french fries
Not forgetting grey greasy mushrooms
With their serried flaps of skin.
Amiable marsala trickles down the throat,
Succulent hunks of mottled meat
Squirm and ooze in the gorge.

Meringue glacé
Sweetness and light on stainless steel —
Crisp beige meringues cemented together
With real dairy cream, tepid
Against the dollop of strawberry ice.

Coffee
Thick china cup and saucer,
Hot, black, reflective liquid,
Cream, sugar crystals, tongue tang.

You owe me £3.

JEREMY THOMAS

It's not easy to describe the taste of things, though advertisers often try. Here is an advertisement for English Cheese, in which the different kinds of cheese are described. A lot of the description deals with texture — the way the cheese feels to our sense of touch — but look carefully at the ways taste is described. No doubt you will have eaten some of these cheeses and know what they taste like.

ENGLISH CHEDDAR: Our first and favourite cheese, firm and nutty.
ENGLISH CHESHIRE: Loosely textured, a fresh, slightly salty taste.
STILTON: A true blue cheese — a rich, full flavour.
DOUBLE GLOUCESTER: The taste's mellow and the texture's firm.
LEICESTER: A russet cheese. Often eaten as a dessert.
DERBY: A smooth white cheese: a smooth mild taste.
CAERPHILLY: White, silky and subtle.
LANCASHIRE: Clean-tasting and crumbly.
WENSLEYDALE: A sweet and creamy cheese from York-shire.

The meaning of some of the description is quite clear — 'Slightly salty', for instance, and 'sweet' (but *how* sweet?), and 'mild' presumably means that the flavour isn't too strong. But what do you think is meant by 'nutty', 'fresh', 'rich', 'full', 'mellow', 'smooth', and 'clean-tasting', when applied to the taste of cheese? Choose a couple of these and try to explain.

An advertisement for pickle describes its taste as 'tangy, fruity.' What does this mean? What sort of fruit would you expect it to taste of? — or isn't this what it means?

Now look at this description of a breakfast cereal:

'Spoonful after spoonful of nut brown crisps with a deep rich malt flavour. Specially baked to keep just the right crispness in milk, right through to the last delicious bite . . .'

Again you'll notice that much of the description is about texture. But how does a word like 'brown' help to describe the taste? 'Malt flavour' means it tastes of malt; what difference do the words 'deep' and 'rich' make to the meaning?

Try writing a similar advertisement for some food you particularly like or dislike.

A SHERBET LEMON

The sweet is the shape of a rugby ball on two sides, the two sides being covered by hundreds of tiny pimples. The other sides have no pattern.

When held up to the light the edges glint a brighter yellow than the centre, which is dull because the sherbet is imprisoned there. My fingers are covered with stickiness. It smells very sweet, in the way that an air freshener does.

In my mouth I suck it; it is sugary sweet. I press it against the roof of my mouth. I feel the rough surface digging in. I feel the sweet with my tongue and roll it about. The sweet becomes sharp and hot. My tongue detects a sharp edge, which is a fault. Some sherbet spills out of it. The sherbet is very bitter and makes my body shiver for a second. It is like having tonic water after chocolate.

Two cracks have formed. The sweet is much smaller. The two cracks run into each other and get larger until I can probe into the centre of the sweet and get at the rest of the sherbet with my tongue. On contact with the sherbet, my tongue jumps up and is pressed on to the roof of my mouth. It is like having an electric shock. The sherbet burns into my cheek like an acid.

The sweet is now thin and brittle. It is snapped in two by my tongue. The new edges soon become rounded, and the small flakes dissolve away in my saliva.

I press my tongue round my sticky lips and lick my fingers. The taste lingers for a few minutes and then dies.

TIMOTHY BOURNE

The boy who wrote this description of a Sherbet Lemon wrote it while he was actually eating the sweet. How can you tell? Is there anything in his description that sounds just right — or, for that matter, anything that seems wrong to you?

Now get a sweet of your own — try to make it an interesting one to eat — and write about it. Take your time: look at it and smell it first, before you put it it into your mouth. Don't crunch it up and swallow it right away; suck it gently and separate how it tastes at first from how it tastes later. What does it feel like in your mouth?

HOT CAKE
(*Translated from the Chinese of Shu Hsi*)

Winter has come; fierce is the cold;
In the sharp morning air new-risen we meet.
Rheum freezes in the nose;
Frost hangs about the chin.
For hollow bellies, for chattering teeth and shivering knees
What better than hot cake?
Soft as the down of spring,
Whiter than autumn wool!

Dense and swift the steam
Rises, swells and spreads.
Fragrance flies through the air,
Is scattered far and wide,
Steals down along the wind and wets
The covetous mouth of passer-by.
Servants and grooms
Throw sidelong glances, munch the empty air.
They lick their lips who serve;
While lines of envious lackeys by the wall
Stand dryly swallowing.

ARTHUR WALEY

This poem is less about the *taste* of hot cake than about the *idea* of it, but though he gives little idea of the taste, he does give a good idea of the texture and feel (lines 7 and 8 especially). Why should the *feel* of hot cake be important in this poem? Why does he spend so long describing the cold morning?

What would you particularly like to eat, or drink, on a cold day? Write about the good taste and feel of it, and don't forget to mention the coldness of the day. If you prefer, write about something you like on a hot day.

● Here is the section on Boiled Eggs from Mrs Beeton's *All About Cookery*.

Boiling eggs is a simple job, but not everyone does it perfectly. There are three ways of doing it; a good cook finds the method that suits her best, and sticks to it.

Method 1. Bring to the boil sufficient water to cover the eggs. Gently place the eggs in the water, set the egg-timer, or make a note of the time, and cook from 3–4$\frac{1}{2}$ min., according to taste. Take out the eggs, tap each lightly, once, with the back of a spoon, and serve.

Method 2. Put the eggs into a pan containing cold water and bring to the boil. When boiling-point is reached, start timing. Cooking will take a little less time than with Method 1.

Method 3. This method is, in effect, coddling, and it produces an egg with a softer white than if actually boiled. Have a pan of boiling water ready, put in the eggs, cover the pan and turn off the heat. Let the pan stand for 6–8 min., according to the degree of softness required.

Which of these methods do you think is the easiest? Say why you think so.

Which of the instructions did you find easiest to read and understand? Were there any sentences that you found difficult to follow? Were there any sentences that could have been put in a clearer or better way? (Find one, and rewrite it so that it is easier to read.)

The way in which recipes and instructions are written has some-times been used by poets in poems which are not really recipes or instructions. Here, for example, is a poem by Philip Oakes called *The Tea Ceremony*.

First warm the pot, making sure
That the water is boiling. Measure the tea,
And then take the pot to the kettle, never the
Kettle to the pot; observe procedure.
Each household has its god or demon
To placate, and today
Is a good time to start. Do it this way.
Offer a choice of milk or lemon,
Either will do. The Japanese
Make a ritual of drinking tea,
Scalding each leaf singly,
Watching their lives unfold. Our way is
Less finicky, but just as meaningful.
Pledging fragments, we redeem the whole.

For the first four lines, at least, you might think that this was just a recipe for making tea; it is only later that it becomes clear that the poem has another meaning too. Here is another poem about making tea. In the way it is written it is less like a recipe, but it is quite good advice on making tea!

ON MAKING TEA

The water bubbles
Should become happy;
Not angry.

The tea leaves
Should become excited;
But not violently so.

The pouring of the water
On the leaves
Should be a conception;
Not a confusion.

The union of the tea and water
Should be allowed to dream;
But not to sleep.

Now follows some moments of rest.

The tea is then gently poured
Into simple, clean containers,
And served before smiling
And understanding friends.

R. L. WILSON

Now write a recipe or some instructions of your own, either as a poem or in prose. It could be a real recipe for something simple like boiling eggs or making tea, or instructions for making a bed or mending a puncture, or, if you prefer, instructions for 'How to Walk' or 'How to Wake Up' or something even more unlikely!

Here is an extract from James Joyce's *Ulysses*, in which Leopold Bloom is getting the breakfast for his wife Mollie, who is still in bed.

Mr Leopold Bloom ate with relish the inner organs of beasts and fowls. He liked thick giblet soup, nutty gizzards, a stuffed roast heart, liver slices fried with crust crumbs, fried hencod's roes. Most of all he liked mutton kidneys which gave to his palate a fine tang of faintly scented urine.

Kidneys were in his mind as he moved about the kitchen softly, righting her breakfast things on the humpy tray. Gelid light and air were in the kitchen but out of doors gentle summer morning everywhere. Made him feel a bit peckish.

The coals were reddening.

Another slice of bread and butter; three, four: right. She didn't like her plate full. Right. He turned from the tray, lifted the kettle off the hob and set it sideways on the fire. It sat there, dull and squat, its spout stuck out. Cup of tea soon. Good. Mouth dry. The cat walked stiffly round a leg of the table with tail on high.

— Mkgnao!

— O, there you are, Mr Bloom said, turning from the fire.

The cat mewed in answer and stalked again stiffly round a leg of the table, mewing. Just how she stalks over my writing table. Prr. Scratch my head. Prr.

Mr Bloom watched curiously, kindly, the lithe black form. Clean to see: the gloss of her sleek hide, the white button under the butt of her tail, the green flashing eyes. He bent down to her, his hands on his knee.

— Milk for the pussens, he said.

— Mrkgnao! the cat cried.

They call them stupid. They understand what we say better than we understand them. She understands all she wants to. Vindictive too. Wonder what I look like to her. Height of a tower? No, she can jump me.

— Afraid of the chickens she is, he said mockingly. Afraid of the chookchooks. I never saw such a stupid pussens as the pussens.

Cruel. Her nature. Curious mice never squeal. Seem to like it.

— Mrkrgnao! the cat said loudly.

She blinked up out of her avid shameclosing eyes, mewing plaintively and long, showing him her milkwhite teeth. He watched the dark eyeslits narrowing with greed till her eyes were green stone. Then he went to the dresser, took the jug Hanlon's milkman had just filled for him poured warm-bubbled milk on a saucer and set it slowly on the floor.

— Gurrhr! she cried, running to lap.

Look at the first paragraph. All the things Mr Bloom likes to eat are quite edible, and many people enjoy them. What makes them sound so unpleasant? How do words like 'thick' and 'nutty' (line 2) help this effect?

In *Ulysses*, James Joyce tries to give an idea of the complete thoughts of the characters, just in the way they think them, and you can see this here. Notice the way Bloom moves from one thought to another — can you see why? Notice, too, the way he gives himself instructions at the beginning of the fourth paragraph. Have you ever talked to yourself like this?

The cat says something slightly different each time; can you explain the difference? What do you notice about the way Bloom speaks to the cat?

Using a similar style as far as you can, write about getting a meal, or getting up early, or any other activity that you do on your own. Try to bring in all the thoughts that come to you while doing it.

If you have time, give an account of the things you like eating particularly in a paragraph starting with your own name:—'John Harris ate with great relish . . .'

●   We would all think of food in a very different light if we were starving or in a prison camp of some kind. In this extract from *One Day in the Life of Ivan Denisovich*, by Alexander Solzhenitszyn, we read about the way Shukhov is accustomed to eating.

Shukhov pulled his spoon out of his boot. His little treasure. It had been with him his whole time in the North, he'd cast it with his own hands out of aluminium wire and it was embossed with the words 'Ust-Izhma 1944'.

Then he removed his hat from his clean-shaven head — however cold it might be, he could never bring himself to eat with his hat on — and stirred the cold skilly, taking a

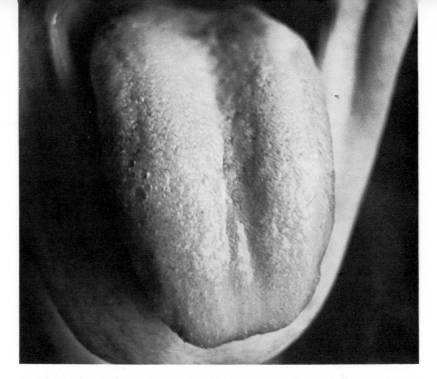

quick look to see what kind of helping they'd given him. An average one. They hadn't ladled it from the top of the cauldron, but they hadn't ladled it from the bottom either. Fetiukov was the sort who when he was looking after someone else's bowl took the potatoes from it.

The only good thing about skilly was that it was hot, but Shukhov's portion had grown quite cold. However, he ate it with his usual slow concentration. No need to hurry, not even for a house on fire. Sleep apart, the only time a prisoner lives for himself is ten minutes in the morning at breakfast, five minutes over dinner and five at supper.

The skilly was the same every day. Its composition depended on the kind of vegetables provided that winter. Nothing but salted carrots last year, which meant that from September to June the skilly was plain carrot. This year it was black cabbage. The most nourishing time of the year was June: then all the vegetables came to an end and were replaced by groats. The worst time was July: then they shredded nettles into the pot.

The little fish were more bone than flesh: the flesh had been boiled off the bone and had disintegrated, leaving a few remnants on head and tail. Without neglecting a single fish-scale or particle of flesh on the brittle skeleton, Shukhov went on champing his teeth and sucking the bones, spitting the remains on the table. He ate everything — the gills, the tail, the eyes when they were still in their sockets but not when they'd been boiled out and floated in the bowl separately — great fish-eyes! Not then. The others laughed at him for that.

This morning Shukhov economized. As he hadn't returned to the hut he hadn't drawn his rations, so he ate his break-fast without bread. He'd eat the bread later. Might even be better that way.

After the skilly there was magara porridge. It had grown cold too, and had set in a solid lump. Shukhov broke it up into pieces. It wasn't only that the porridge was cold — it was tasteless when hot, and left you no sense of having filled your belly. Just grass, except that it was yellow, and looked like millet. They'd got the idea of serving it instead of cereals from the Chinese, it was said. When boiled, a bowlful of it weighed nearly a pound. Not much of a porridge but that was what it passed for.

Licking his spoon and tucking it back into his boot, Shukhov put on his hat and went to the sick-bay.

The food advertisements on pages 76 and 77 suggested the importance of the texture and smell in our appreciation of food. How would you react to Shukhov's meal?

See if you can describe the *feel* of the following things:

(a) Chewing up a little fish or any sort of fish bone.
(b) Sucking a fish skeleton for the last drop of flavour.
(c) Having a bone stuck between your teeth.
(d) Biting into a lump of cold porridge.
(e) Finding you have a fish's eye in your mouth which you can't swallow

Think of something which you always have to eat *carefully*, either because it has little bones or pips in it or because there are bits of gristle, fat or skin that you don't like. Write about eating it, describing in detail how you tackle it, and what you feel about the bits you are trying to avoid eating. Have you ever been *made* to eat something you really hated? How did you cope with it?

THE SENSE OF TOUCH

The impact of the sense of touch in writing — walking barefoot over different surfaces — the feel of things to our hands and fingertips — dentist and hairdressers — the feel of your body and your clothes — in a butcher's shop.

In the last chapter we saw how important the sense of touch is to our appreciation of food, and how we are sometimes put off something because of the thought of the feel of it — this is why some people don't like tripe or shellfish.

The sense of touch is also very important when you are describing something — if you can get your reader to imagine what something feels like you are doing well. Sometimes it is even possible to make the reader wince — perhaps *you* did when you read about the fishes' eyes in the last piece!

Normally we think of the sense of touch as something centred in our fingertips, but of course we have feeling in most parts of our bodies, and the first part of this chapter deals with the feel of walking, especially in bare feet.

The shepherd in the next poem is an African shepherd, who would normally walk barefoot. Here he is bathing his feet.

YOUNG SHEPHERD BATHING HIS FEET

Only the short, broad, splayed feet
Moved . . .

Feet that had trodden over
Soft soil,
Sand,
Ploughed veld,
Mountain rocks
And along narrow tracks,
On Winter clay and
Dust of
Summer roads . . .

The short, broad, splayed feet
Moved
In and out . . .

The stumpy toes stretched wide
Apart
And closed together
Then opened wide . . .

In ecstasy.

PETER CLARKE

Wriggle your toes inside your shoes, stretching them wide apart and closing them together, like the boy in the poem. What does it feel like? What can you feel between your toes?

Think what it would feel to walk barefoot over 'Soft soil, Sand, Ploughed veld, Mountain rocks And along narrow tracks, On Winter clay and Dust of Summer roads.' Choose two and describe the feel of them.

Here's another extract from *Ulysses* about a man walking along a beach. Although he is wearing boots, we get a good idea what it would feel like to walk barefoot.

The grainy sand had gone from under his feet. His boots trod again a damp crackling mast, razorshells, squeaking pebbles, that on the unnumbered pebbles beats, wood sieved by the shipworm, lost Armada. Unwholesome sand-flats waited to suck his treading soles, breathing upward sewage breath. He coasted them, walking warily. A porter-bottle stood up, stogged to its waist, in the cakey sand. A sentinel: isle of dreadful thirst. Broken hoops on the shore; at the land a maze of dark cunning nets; farther away chalkscrawled back-doors and on the higher beach a dryingline with two crucified shirts. Ringsend: wigwams of brown steersmen and master mariners. Human shells.

JAMES JOYCE

You may find some of the ideas here difficult to follow, but notice the way all the things he mentions help to create the effect.
Imagine what it would feel like to walk barefoot

(a) over pebbles or stones (What noise would they make?)
(b) over dry and powdery sand (What prints would your feet make?)
(c) over hard, damp sand
(d) over very wet sand (How would this be different from (c)?)
(e) into the cold sea.

Now put all these ideas together to write a description of walking into the sea. If you like, you can continue your description until you are right in the water. Take your time, and imagine each stage carefully.

● But when we think of the sense of touch, we usually think of our hands, and particularly our fingertips. The next poem is about pulling up weeds — something you do with your hands.

WEED PULLER

Under the concrete benches,
Hacking at black hairy roots, —
Those lewd monkey-tails hanging from drainholes, —
Digging into the soft rubble underneath,
Webs and weeds,
Grubs and snails and sharp sticks,
Or yanking tough fern-shapes,
Coiled green and thick, like dripping smilax,
Tugging all day at perverse life:
The indignity of it! —
With everything blooming above me,
Lilies, pale-pink cyclamen, roses,
Whole fields lovely and inviolate, —
Me down in that fetor of weeds,
Crawling on all fours,
Alive, in a slippery grave.

THEODORE ROETHKE

You get a good idea of the *feel* of weeding from this, and if you look closely at the words he uses you can see why. Notice the strong words like 'hacking' and 'digging', which make you feel you're actually doing it, and the words which tell you what things feel like — '*hairy* roots', '*soft* rubble', for instance. What other examples can you find?

Imagine the feel of the following, and describe two of them:

(a) Digging with your hands into earth or damp sand.
(b) Letting dry sand run through your fingers.
(c) Mixing flour or making pastry or dough with your hands.
(d) Picking flowers (what sort?) or breaking a springy stick in your hands.
(e) Taking off a wet sock.
(f) Stroking a dog, cat, or horse, or a snake, if you've actually handled one.
(g) Peeling an apple, orange or peach.

Now write about feeling for something you can't see — trying to find something that has fallen down the back of a chair, or behind a cupboard, or something at the bottom of a bag or pocket.

● It's easy enough to write corny old descriptions of waiting in dentists' waiting rooms, but think for a moment of what you feel *in your mouth* from the moment the dentist tells you to 'Open wide' to the time when he tells you to 'Rinse out'. Here's part of a story by William Sansom to help you:

But the dentist had only walked once over to the nurse before he was back again prodding, this time nonchalantly, without asking what was felt, and before Pemberton could speak or even make his delaying noise, a deep groaned guttural vowel, a hand was over his mouth concealing — kind conjuror — the wink of a bright instrument, a white arm was braced dark against the sky, he heard inside his ears a crunching, felt nothing, saw the arm arc swiftly back to place something on the tray, then instantly brace back again, brace, crunch, arc, brace, crunch, arc, five times, and so expertly that Pemberton could make no sound, his mouth in any case immobilized wide, and then his head was gently pushed forward and the dentist, with the grave, knowing smile reserved to his calling, was saying: 'Would you spit, please?' and out of his mouth into the glass bowl with its little circular hiss of water he saw his blood drop, not with horror, but with a beautiful relief. He had felt nothing. Condemned, he had been reprieved. He looked up at the dentist with worship of such dexterity, with love. This passed quickly to a sensation of personal bravery. 'I got through.' 'It was nothing.' He felt like a man who has pulled somebody from the Thames and slips anonymous away from his congratulators.

When you've got your mouth wide open it's not easy to talk, or swallow, or to make a noise. What sort of a noise would you make to attract attention in this position? What would it feel like to make it?

What is the dentist doing to Pemberton in this passage? What is the crunching he hears inside his ears? What does the arm place on the tray?

What do the various instruments feel like inside your mouth?

Now here's a poem about a boy having a haircut.

ALEX AT THE BARBER'S

He is having his hair cut. Towels are tucked
About his chin, his mop scalped jokingly.
The face in the mirror is his own face.

The barber moves and chats about the green
And methylated violet, snipper-snips,
Puts scissors down, plugs in a plaited flex,

And like a surgeon with his perfumed hands
Presses the waiting skull and shapes the base.
He likes having his hair cut, and the man

Likes cutting it. The radio drones on.
The eyes in the mirror are his own eyes.
While the next chair receives the Demon Blade,

A dog-leg razor nicks a sideburn here;
As from a sofa there a sheet is whisked
And silver pocketed. The doorbell pings.

The barber, frowning, grips the ragged fringe
And slowly cuts. Upon the speckled sheet
The bits fall down and now his hair is cut.

JOHN FULLER

At the hairdresser's, unlike the dentist's, you have a mirror so that you can see what he is doing. Would you prefer to have a mirror at the dentist's? Why?

In this poem the writer mentions quite a number of sounds. What sounds do you associate with being at the hairdresser's?

What do the following feel like? Describe two of them.

(a) Scissors cutting your hair.
(b) Hair clippers — hand or electric.
(c) A razor being used to taper your hair, or to shape your sideburns.
(d) A hair dryer after a shampoo.
(e) Hair down your neck.

Write your own description of a visit to the dentist or to the hairdresser. Concentrate especially on what is done to your hair or teeth and try to get the exact feel of everything that happens.

● Touch sensations are coming from almost all parts of your body — inside as well as outside — all the time, but when you get used to the feel of something you stop noticing it; so normally you don't notice many of them. In the next extract, from his short story *The Peaches*, Dylan Thomas is hiding from his friend, and, as he crouches hidden and silent among the undergrowth, he is suddenly aware of the feel of his body.

On my haunches, eager and alone, casting an ebony shadow, with the Gorsehill jungle swarming, the violent, impossible birds and fishes leaping, hidden under four-stemmed flowers

the height of horses, in the early evening in a dingle near Carmarthen, my friend Jack Williams invisibly near me, I felt all my young body like an excited animal surrounding me, the torn knees bent, the bumping heart, the long heat and depth between the legs, the sweat prickling in the hands, the tunnels down to the eardrums, the little balls of dirt between the toes, the eyes in the sockets, the tucked-up voice, the blood racing, the memory around and within flying, jumping, swimming, and waiting to pounce. There, playing Indians in the evening, I was aware of me myself in the exact middle of a living story, and my body was my adventure and my name. I sprang with excitement and scrambled up through the scratching brambles again.

Some of these things need careful imagining, but it is quite easy to imagine the 'sweat prickling in the hands', 'the little balls of dirt between the toes', and the feeling of having your knees bent up under you. What do you think he means by 'the tucked-up voice'?

Sit quite still, and notice the following:

(a) The feel of the chair and the floor underneath you.
(b) The feel of your clothes, especially around your waist, your shoulders and neck.
(c) The feel of your lungs breathing and your heart beating.
(d) The feel of your hair (Can you feel it growing? What about your fingernails?)

Now write about what it feels like to be sitting there inside your body.

If you feel tired, or hungry, what exactly do you feel, and whereabouts in your body do you feel it?

96